CREATIVE COMPANIES

THE STORY OF NIKE

AARON FRISCH

JAICO PUBLISHING HOUSE

Ahmedabad Bangalore Chennai
Delhi Hyderabad Kolkata Mumbai

Published by Jaico Publishing House
A-2 Jash Chambers, 7-A Sir Phirozshah Mehta Road
Fort, Mumbai - 400 001
jaicopub@jaicobooks.com
www.jaicobooks.com

Published in arrangement with
The Creative Company
123 South Broad Street, Mankato, MN 56001, USA

To be sold only in India, Bangladesh, Bhutan,
Pakistan, Nepal, Sri Lanka and the Maldives.

Design and Production by Zeno Design

Photographs by Alamy (Laskowitz), Corbis (Bettmann, Jonathan Ferrey, Wally McNamee, Franck Seguin/TempSport), Getty Images (Andrew D. Bernstein/NBAE, Todd Bigelow/Aurora, Tim Boyle, Clive Brunskill/Allsport, David Cannon, MIKE CLARKE/AFP, Jonathan Ferrey, Mark Dadswell, Jonathan Ferrey, FRANCK FIFE/AFP, Kevin Fleming, Nick Laham, Alan Levenson//Time Life Pictures, Jasper Juinen, Bob Martin/Allsport, Co Rentmeester// Time Life Pictures, Ron Vesely), Oregon Archive

THE STORY OF NIKE
ISBN 978-81-8495-439-5

First Jaico Impression: 2013
Seventh Jaico Impression: 2025

Page design and layouts: Special Effects, Mumbai

Printed by
Trinity Academy For Corporate Training Limited, Mumbai

CREATIVE COMPANIES

THE STORY OF NIKE

LeBron James streaks down the basketball court and soars to the rim for a slam dunk, his personalized Nike shoes propelling him several feet off the floor. Dressed in bright-colored Nike tights and top, Serena Williams tosses a tennis ball over her head and fires a scorching serve at her opponent. Tiger Woods stands over a golf ball with a tiny curved logo on it, then, flawlessly swinging a Nike iron, launches the ball 200 yards (183 m), narrowly missing the cup. No matter the sport, Nike and its unmistakable "Swoosh" logo are likely to be there. This giant of a corporation today towers above all competitors in the sports apparel industry, but Nike began almost five decades ago with nothing but a young runner and a dream.

1

A Blue Ribbon Beginning

In the early 1960s, a Stanford Business School graduate student named Phil Knight was assigned a term paper on how he would create a new company. The Oregon native, who had run competitively in high school and college, settled on an idea of personal interest: how to design and sell track shoes.

After researching the industry, Knight was left with an ambitious idea. He thought he really could start his own business by buying low-cost athletic shoes made in Japan and selling them in America. "I had determined when I wrote that paper," Knight would later say, "that what I wanted to do with my life was to be the best track and field shoe distributor in the United States."

At the time, American companies sold a lot of sneakers—comfortable and inexpensive shoes that people wore for leisure. German manufacturers, especially Adidas, were known to make the best athletic shoes. Most serious track and field athletes wore Adidas, but Knight thought he could compete against the German outfitters by selling shoes for less.

On Thanksgiving Day in 1962, Knight boarded a plane for Japan. There, he visited a sporting goods store and saw a pair of running shoes with the brand name "Tiger," manufactured by a company called Onitsuka. Knight took a train to the city of Kobe, where he met with executives of the company, telling them that he was a shoe importer from the U.S. When asked the name of his company, which didn't yet exist, Knight said the first thing that popped into his head: Blue Ribbon Sports.

Knight's first order, five pairs of white-and-blue leather Tiger shoes, didn't arrive in the U.S. until more than a year later. Knight and Bill Bowerman, his former track coach at the University of Oregon, each chipped in $500 to import more shoes. Bowerman agreed to promote the shoes to college athletes; Knight would handle everything else. Less than a year later, Knight had sold 1,300 pairs of running shoes out of the trunk of his car at regional track meets, supporting his fledgling business by working as an accountant.

In 1965, Knight met Jeff Johnson, a former running rival, at a track meet and approached him about promoting Tiger shoes, offering an advance of $400 and an income based on commission. Johnson was not particularly interested, but, in need of work, he agreed to sell them on a part-

Phil Knight was 24 years old when he launched the athletic shoe company that would become Nike time basis. In 1966, he sold so many shoes that Knight hired him as the company's first full-time employee. Johnson inadvertently pushed Blue Ribbon Sports into the apparel business when he started handing out T-shirts with the Tiger name printed across the front to promote the shoes. The T-shirts became so popular that Johnson and Knight decided to sell them as well, and they opened their first retail store along busy Pico Boulevard in Santa Monica, California.

While Knight handled the business and Johnson handled the sales, Bill Bowerman provided much of the young company's inspiration. Bowerman

Nike cofounder Bill Bowerman (right) coached track
and field at the University of Oregon for 24 years

was widely regarded as the finest track coach in America, and his running program at the University of Oregon was legendary. His reputation only grew in 1967 when he co-authored the book *Jogging: A Physical Fitness Program for All Ages,* which sold more than one million copies. The book explained how jogging could strengthen a person's heart and lungs, burn body fat, and build endurance, and all that was required was a good pair of shoes. As a coach, Bowerman pushed his runners hard—"Nobody ever remembers number two," he liked to say—and was always looking for a competitive edge. He began tinkering with footwear designs, hoping to make Tiger shoes lighter and better-performing than anything else on the market.

In 1968, Bowerman designed a shoe that combined the best features of all

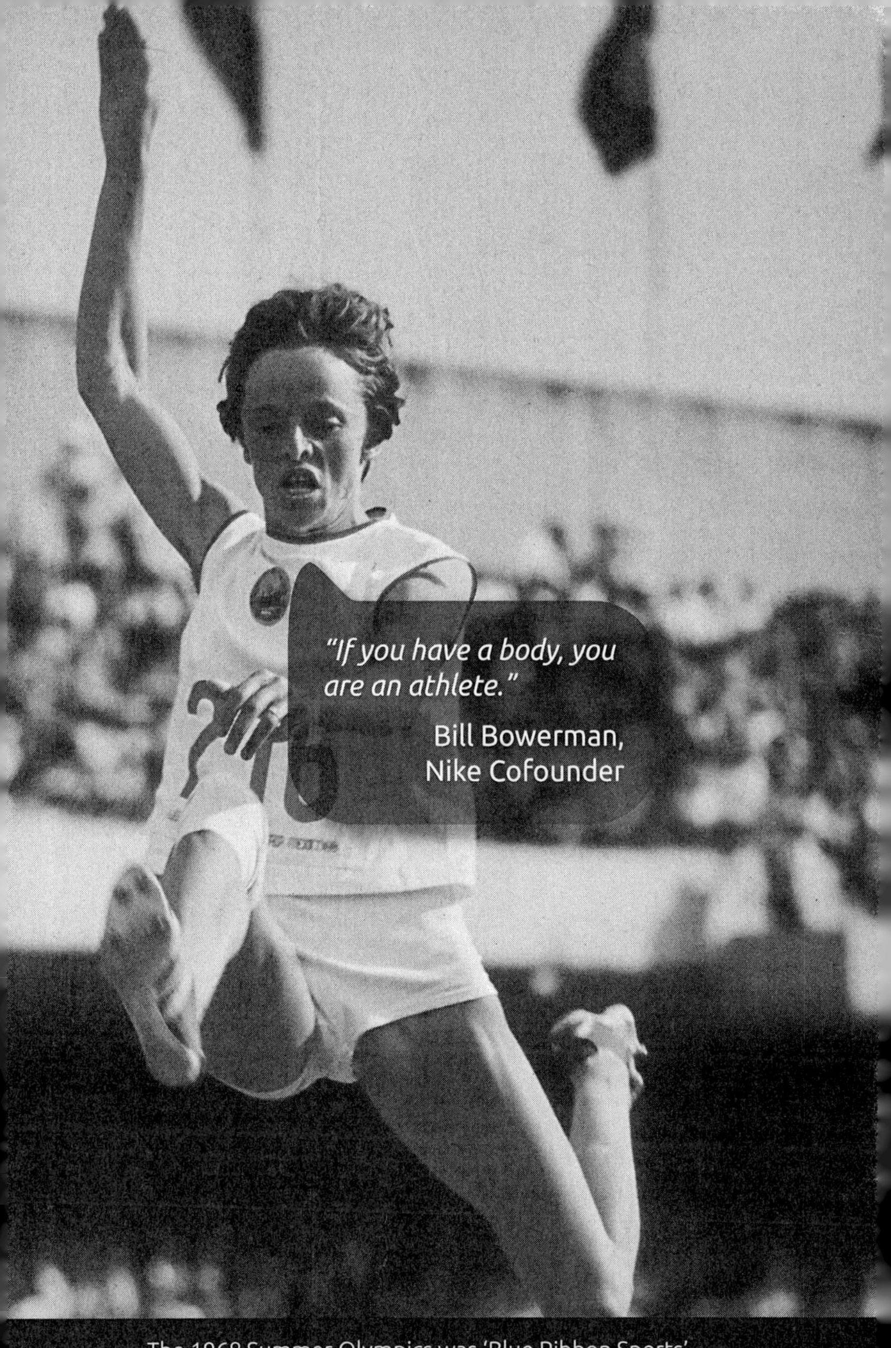

The 1968 Summer Olympics was 'Blue Ribbon Sports' first big chance to test its shoe designs

The Man behind Nike

Philip Hampson Knight grew up in a suburb of Portland, Oregon. Known to his childhood friends as "Buck," he enjoyed athletics but wasn't big enough to excel at football or basketball. As a teen, he took up running instead. When he enrolled at the University of Oregon, Knight joined the track team, coached by a passionate running enthusiast named Bill Bowerman. The coach would later help Knight start the Blue Ribbon Sports company. Knight seemed an unlikely leader to build up a multi-billion-dollar company—he was quiet and hated speaking in public ("I still get real nervous when I go in front of more than two people," he said in 2005)—but he had a knack for surrounding himself with talented executives. By 2007, Knight remained company chairman, and his stake in Nike made him one of the wealthiest men in the U.S., with a net worth of about $8 billion.

the running shoes he had seen up to that point, including fuller "heel to toe" cushioning. He showed it to executives at Onitsuka, who liked the design and manufactured the shoe just in time for the 1968 Summer Olympics in Mexico City. Blue Ribbon named it the Cortez, and it became one of the best-selling shoes that Bowerman and Knight would market as partners.

Bowerman next suggested to Onitsuka that it make a running shoe from nylon. The Japanese manufacturer elaborated on his idea, making a rubber-soled marathon shoe with a thin layer of foam sandwiched between two sheets of nylon. The shoe was lighter than anything made of leather or canvas. The Tiger Marathon, as it was called, changed the athletic shoe market forever.

Blue Ribbon Sports secured an exclusive contract to sell the Tiger Marathon, and in 1969, revenues reached $400,000. One year later, the company earned $1 million, but it also faced difficulties. Although sales were good, Blue Ribbon's operating costs had soared. In addition,

Onitsuka sometimes had difficulty shipping the larger orders on time, and customers became annoyed by the delays. Facing these complications, Knight and Bowerman soon decided to create their own brand.

2

A Company with Sole

In 1971, Blue Ribbon Sports' co-founders designed a new shoe, but they needed cash to manufacture it. To generate the necessary funds, they decided to sell part of the company. By the fall of 1971, investors owned about 35 percent of Blue Ribbon Sports.

Buoyed by the added funds, the partners were soon promoting a new line of shoes they called Nike. (The name, a reference to the Greek goddess of victory, came to Jeff Johnson in a dream and replaced Phil Knight's original choice, "Dimension 6.")

In June 1971, Blue Ribbon's first shoes bearing the Nike name and its unique "Swoosh" logo went on sale. Unfortunately, there was a major glitch. The shoes were made in the warm climate of Mexico, and no one had tested them in the cold weather of the northern U.S. The soles cracked, and the shoes had to be sold at a reduced price. The company had manufactured 10,000 pairs, and almost all were sold for a mere $7.95.

In October of that year, Knight flew to Japan with a new line of credit from a Japanese trading company called Nissho Iwai. With this credit, Knight ordered 6,000 pairs of the popular Tiger Cortez, but now he requested that Onitsuka put the Nike logo on every pair. On the same trip, he purchased basketball and wrestling shoes, as well as casual street shoes, from other Japanese manufacturers.

As Blue Ribbons's operations and staff grew in the early 1970s, Knight sought out employees with a flair for creative thinking and a nonconformist attitude. He enjoyed hearing his employees talk sports, and loud arguments were a common—and even encouraged—part of meetings at the Nike workplace. One observer who stopped by the company's offices remarked, "Nike is like high school, only with money."

In 1972, the U.S. Men's Track and Field Olympic Trials were held in Eugene, Oregon, and athletes from all over America came to compete for a chance to make the Olympic team. The event was significant to Nike for two reasons. First, a fiery runner from the University of Oregon named Steve Prefontaine, soon to become one of the public faces of the Nike name, emerged as a star. The event also put a spotlight on Blue Ribbon Sports, as the company's shoes could be seen on the feet of many top athletes. Nike shoes were not

Nike's distinctive—and now globally recognized
—Swoosh logo was first introduced in 1971

low-priced the way the first Tiger shoes were, but athletes appreciated the high quality of design and manufacture.

That same year, Bowerman had a shoe design epiphany. One day, he poured some liquid latex into his wife's hot waffle iron. The result was a ruined waffle iron and a solid piece of latex with a square pattern. Bowerman showed the molded sample to Knight, who liked the idea of a textured, latex sole that would give runners and football players better traction while reducing shoe weight. The Waffle outsole was born, and the Waffle Trainer shoe would be unveiled to the public in 1974.

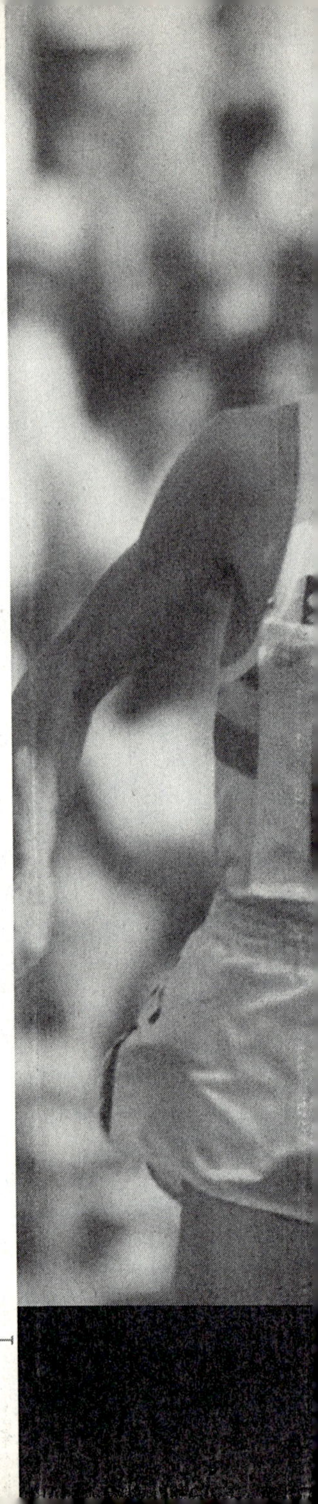

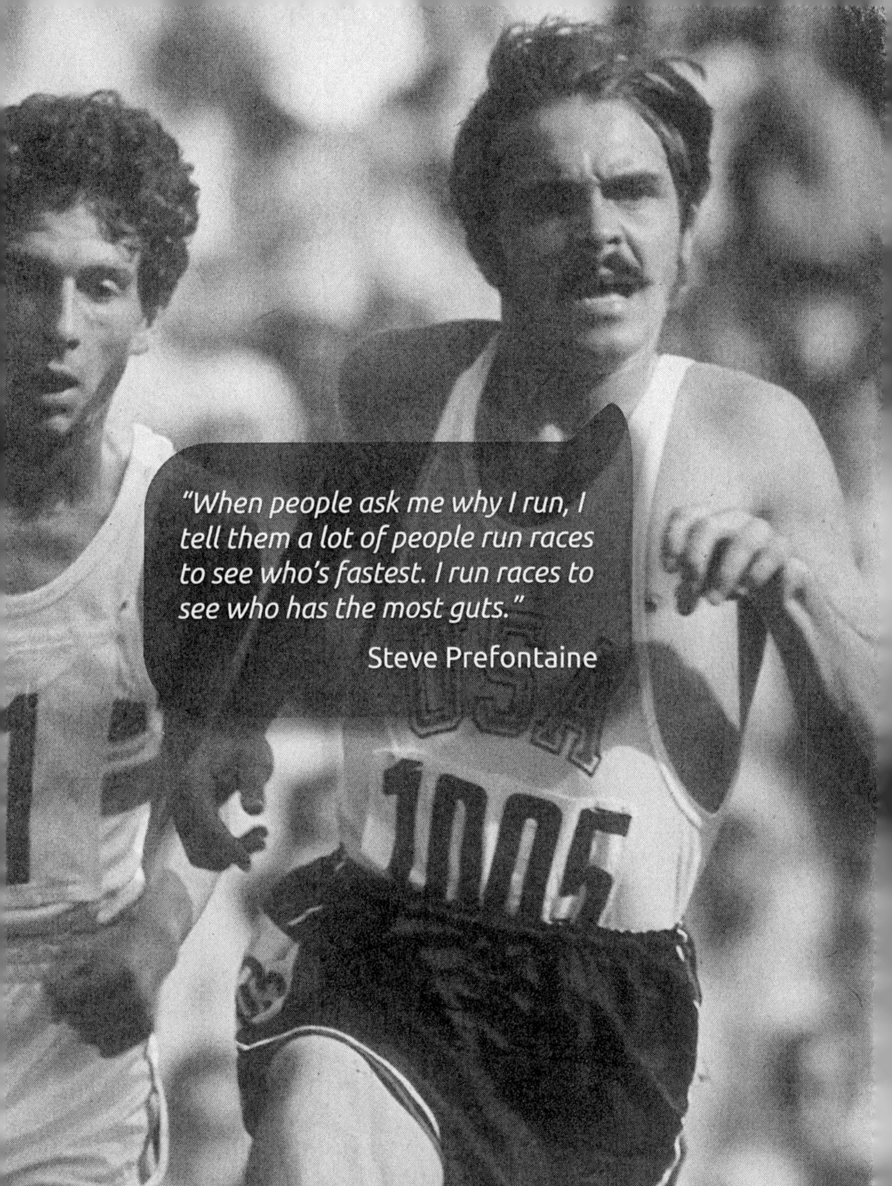

With his aggressive running style,
Steve Prefontaine (right) came to epitomize the Nike athlete

In 1972, Blue Ribbon Sports sold 250,000 pairs of running shoes and 50,000 pairs of basketball shoes. Business was booming, but the company had a problem. When Onitsuka learned that Blue Ribbon was selling Japanese-made shoes other than Tigers, it decided to find other U.S. distributors. Knight filed a lawsuit against Onitsuka in 1973, charging that the manufacturer had broken its contract. Onitsuka countersued, alleging that Blue Ribbon had used the Tiger trademark illegally to push the sales of Nike shoes. At the end of the bitter dispute, a judge allowed both Blue Ribbon Sports and Onitsuka to sell the shoe designs they had worked on together. Only Blue Ribbon, however, could use the model names, such as Cortez.

Blue Ribbon Sports had lost its main Japanese supply line, but Knight

Every year, Nike sponsors the Prefontaine Classic,
a premier track and field meet held at the University of Oregon

Swoosh—the Nike Logo

In 1970, the new Nike line of shoes needed a logo, a symbol that people would associate with the brand. Blue Ribbon Sports executives wanted something that suggested movement and speed and would also set them apart from other shoe companies. Adidas, for example, had three stripes on the arch of its shoes, while Puma had a stripe that ran along the sides. Knight asked Carolyn Davidson, an art student he knew, to come up with several designs. After reviewing her sketches, Knight and his partners finally settled on a logo that resembled a rounded check mark. "I don't love it," Knight admitted, "but maybe it will grow on me." The logo did grow on him. Over time, the symbol (for which Davidson charged $35) became known as the "Swoosh," and it is today one of the most recognizable trademarks in the world.

was confident he could continue to build up the company, partly through endorsements. Steve Prefontaine became Nike's first endorser when Knight and Bowerman agreed in 1973 to pay for his training if he wore their shoes and shorts. Prefontaine was exactly what Nike aspired to represent. With his wild, flowing hair, he cut a unique and instantly recognizable image, and he ran with a rare passion and determination, pushing through pain and fatigue that would have stopped most runners.

"Pre" won several national collegiate championships in the early '70s and was poised for international stardom, but his life and career were cut short when he was killed in a car accident in 1975. At the time of his death, the 24-year-old held seven U.S. track records. Pre was gone, but he would become a legend and a lasting influence at Nike. Not only had his commitment to the brand established Nike as a legitimate sports brand, but his fiery spirit had helped to shape Nike's mission: "To bring inspiration and innovation to every athlete in the world."

By the summer of 1975, Blue Ribbon Sports had signed several top National Basketball Association (NBA) players, including Elvin Hayes and Spencer Haywood, to endorsement deals. Each player received $2,000 a year and a small royalty from profits on Nike basketball shoes. The cost of signing such big-name players to endorsement contracts rose quickly; within a few years, companies would be paying NBA players up to $10,000 to wear their shoes. The sports world was expanding quickly, and the money involved was expanding with it.

3

Jordan and Beyond

In the late 1970s, Blue Ribbon Sports made great strides in shoe design. In 1977, a former NASA engineer named Frank Rudy came up with an idea to reduce the shock of impact when running and jumping on hard pavement. He suggested placing pockets of air inside the shoe's sole to cushion the foot.

The first shoes did not hold up well, the air pockets deflating after a hard jog, but Knight liked the idea, and he added Rudy to the Blue Ribbon payroll and told him to keep experimenting.

Knight and his team introduced a running shoe called the Tailwind in 1979, just after the company name was officially changed to Nike. The Tailwind was very light, and the sole contained tiny sacs filled with gas—a cushioning system that came to be called Nike Air. Athletes could run, jump, and play as hard as they wanted, with less fear of injury, and their shoes would spring back to their original shape.

In 1980, Nike pulled in $269 million and reached a major milestone by replacing Adidas as the most popular athletic shoe in the U.S. Amid this growth, Nike began to sell stock to the public. In Blue Ribbon's earliest years, friends and family members had pitched in $5,000 each when Knight and Bowerman needed money to keep the company going. By the early 1980s, those $5,000 investments had skyrocketed to a value of $3 million each.

Nike shoes were well-represented at the 1980 Olympic Trials, and college baseball and football programs and coaches were now on the Nike payroll as well, being decked out in uniforms and cleats bearing Nike's signature Swoosh. But it was in the professional ranks that the company spent the most money growing the Nike name. In 1978, Nike had signed a young tennis player named John McEnroe for $100,000. McEnroe was the top tennis moneymaker of the day, and even when he wasn't winning, he received considerable media attention due to his flamboyant personality and frequent on-court temper tantrums. In 1981, long-distance runner Alberto Salazar gave Nike free publicity when he set a world marathon record wearing Nikes. By then, Nike's inventory included more than 200 kinds of shoes.

By the mid-1980s, Nike had decided not to pay large numbers of athletes to endorse its shoes; instead, it would entice a small number—the most elite—with huge contracts. In 1984, Nike signed its first megastar, basketball sensation

The Air sole technology developed by Nike in the late 1970s is still used in many of the company's shoes

Michael Jordan. When Jordan left college for the NBA after his junior year, the Chicago Bulls signed him to a five-year, $3-million contract. Nike, confident that it was getting a rare marketing force and a player who would make television highlight reels on a nightly basis, signed the young man to a five-year, $2.5-million deal and created his own personal shoe: the Air Jordan, a reference both to the shoes' cushioning technology and the way that Jordan so effortlessly leaped through the air.

When Jordan took the court for the first time wearing his special red-and-black shoes, the NBA fined the Bulls $1,000 for violating the

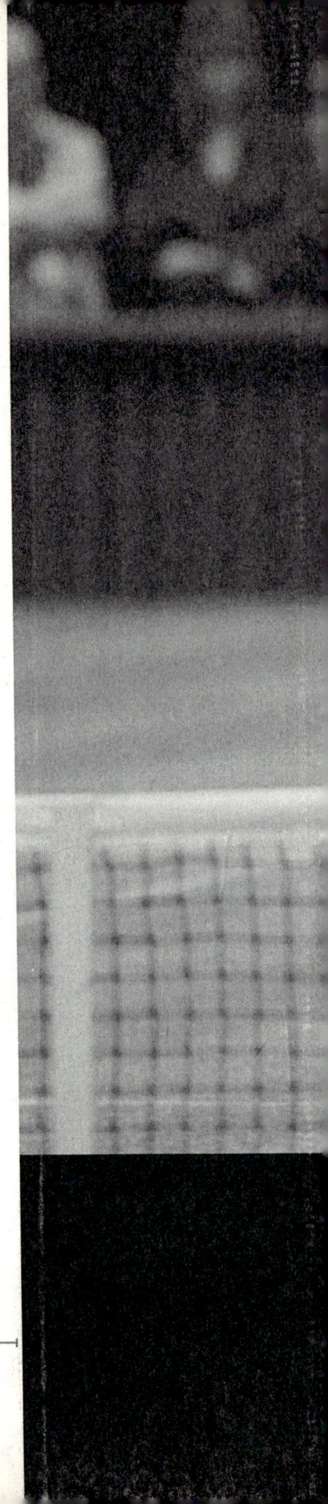

Tennis star John McEnroe was just 19 years old
when he signed an endorsement deal with Nike in 1978.

league's uniform dress code. Nike cleverly seized on the fine as a publicity opportunity, producing a television commercial that showed Jordan bouncing a ball as a voice said: "On September 15, Nike created a revolutionary new basketball shoe. On October 18, the NBA threw them out of the game. Fortunately, the NBA can't keep you from wearing them. Air Jordans from Nike."

As Jordan forged a legacy as the greatest basketball player of all time, Nike grew exponentially. Throughout the 1980s (and '90s), in every year except 1987, Nike shoes would be the top-selling athletic footwear in the world. The

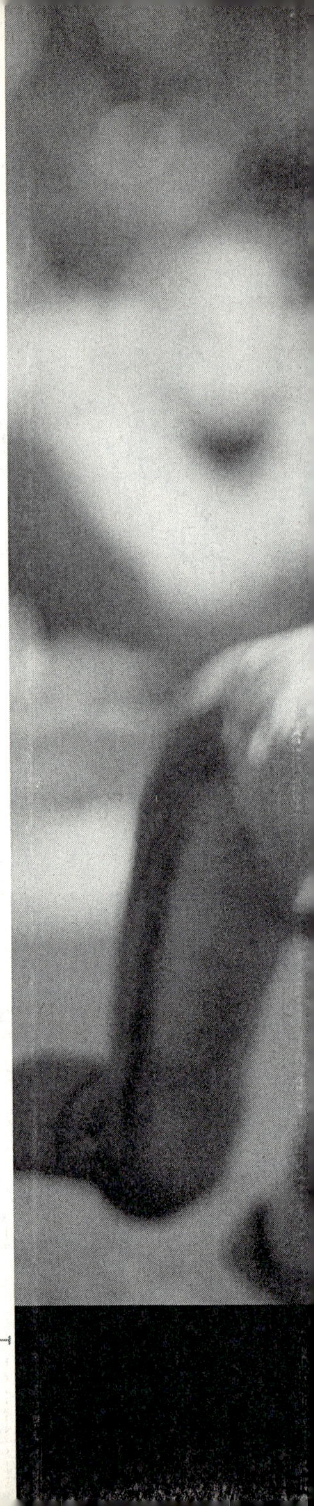

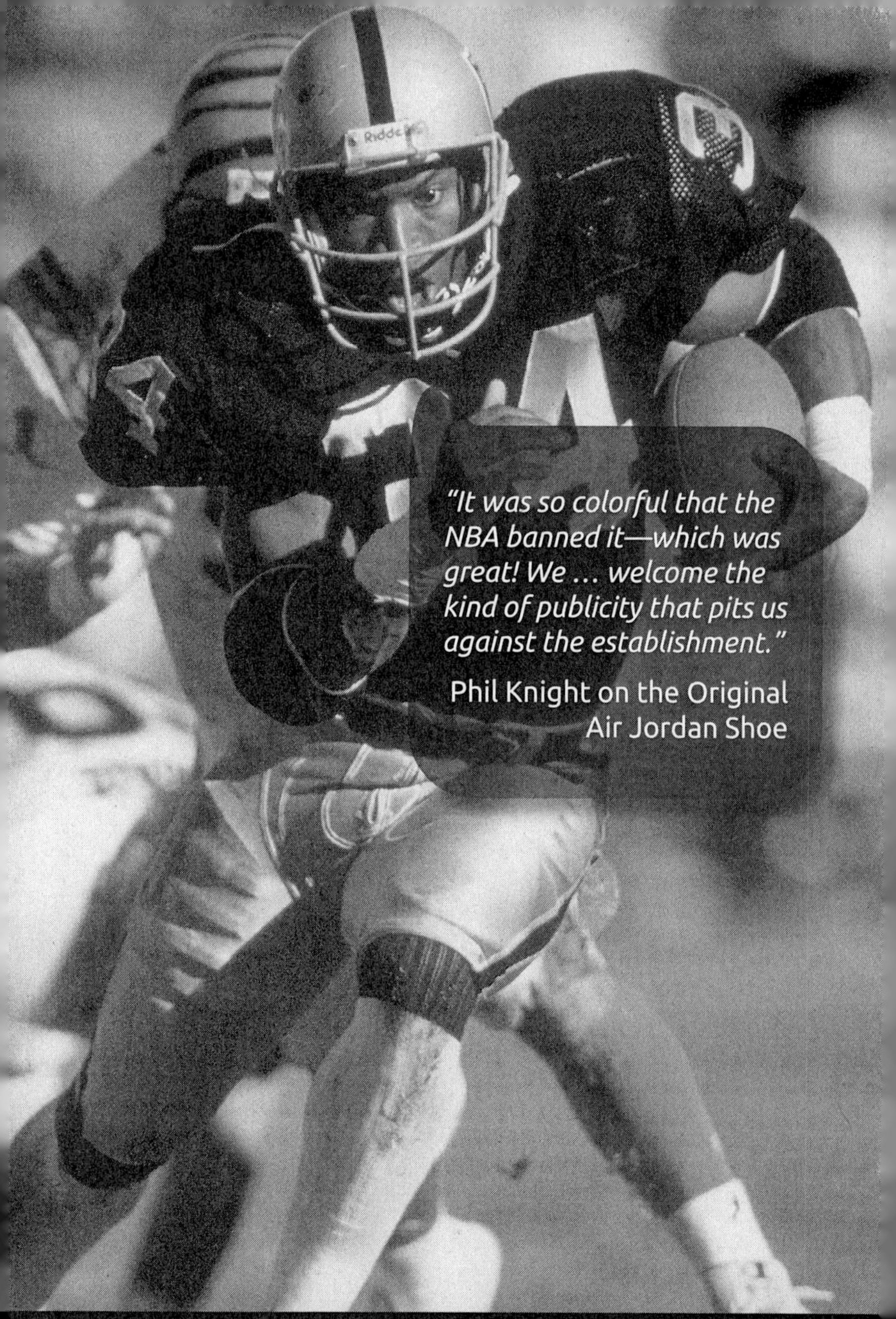

"It was so colorful that the NBA banned it—which was great! We … welcome the kind of publicity that pits us against the establishment."

Phil Knight on the Original Air Jordan Shoe

Although his professional football career lasted only four seasons, Bo Jackson was a huge star for Nike

33
Jazz

Air Jordan

In 1984, Michael Jordan left the University of North Carolina after his junior year to join the Chicago Bulls in the NBA. Nike executives desperately wanted the high-flying young star to wear their shoes, but Jordan actually preferred Adidas, having worn them throughout high school and college. In the end, Nike made him an offer he couldn't turn down: $2.5 million over five years and his own line of Nike basketball shoes, called Air Jordans. Air Jordans, like Jordan himself, were an instant sensation. In 1985, customers bought $130 million worth of the shoes. Jordan went on to play in the NBA for 15 seasons, and Air Jordans—which were redesigned year after year—remained a high-selling product years after he retired. In 2007, Nike released the newest model, the $175 Air Jordan XX2. "There's Michael Jordan," NBA star Magic Johnson once said, "and then there is the rest of us."

1987 stumble was due largely to Nike's failure to recognize the newest trend in fitness, a low-impact type of exercise called aerobics. The company fell into second place that year behind Reebok, whose aerobic shoes sold well. The defeat cast light onto a market that Nike had previously overlooked; up until that time, the vast majority of the company's products and advertisements had been aimed at men. Reebok's surge made it clear that female athletes represented an audience that needed much greater attention.

As Nike responded with expanded footwear and apparel lines for women, it also unveiled a new kind of shoe: the cross-trainer. These shoes were more ruggedly built than running shoes and were more versatile, designed not only for running but for weightlifting or aerobics as well. In 1989, Nike found the perfect spokesman for its cross-trainers: Bo Jackson. A remarkably fast and powerful athlete, Jackson had starred as a baseball outfielder and a football running back at Alabama's Auburn University. He decided to turn professional in baseball in 1986, then went pro in football as well in 1987.

Nike signed Jackson to pitch a shoe called the Air Trainer, creating a wildly successful ad campaign featuring the slogan "Bo Knows" and entertaining commercials that showed Jackson doing everything from playing tennis to running luge. The idea was that Nike's Trainers were the perfect choice for almost any sport, just like Bo. Thanks largely to such successful endorsement decisions, in 1993, *Sporting News* magazine called Phil Knight "the most powerful man in sports."

4

Just Do It

In 1991, Nike became the first sports and fitness company ever to earn more than $3 billion in a year. Then, from 1995 to 1997, the company expanded at an astounding rate. By the end of the 1997 fiscal year, the company had sold more than $9 billion in shoes, clothing, and sports equipment.

Big-name endorsements continued to be responsible for much of this growth and popularity. In 1996, more than a decade after signing Michael Jordan, Nike signed another young sports icon: golfer Tiger Woods. Woods, a man of mixed ethnicity in a game that had long been considered a "white sport," piqued the interest of a new generation of golfers with his spectacular drives and unshakeable focus. Knight paid about $40 million to secure the 20-year-old's endorsement; in 2000, after Woods had won nearly 20 professional tournaments and Nike Golf had been created as an official brand, the contract would be reworked to the tune of $105 million.

Nike built new product lines and marketing campaigns around Woods and other elite athletes such as baseball shortstop Derek Jeter, underscoring an attitude that was distinctly Nike: hardworking, competitive, tough… and fashionable. Many Nike advertisements also featured less-famous athletes—and even ordinary people—with the "Just Do It" slogan to emphasize that anyone could be an athlete. All it took was sweat and dedication. In the mid-1990s, Nike produced a number of ads aimed exclusively at female athletes; one Nike T-shirt bore the slogan, "I am woman. Watch me score."

By the late '90s, Nike was the undisputed king of the sports apparel industry. But the company began to find that its position atop the mountain left it exposed to criticism. Nike prided itself on aggressive advertising, but some critics saw the company's tactics as ruthless and even tacky. For the 1996 Olympics, for example, Nike won the bidding rights to be the official outfitter of the U.S. Track and Field Team and soon revealed track suits that had Swooshes instead of stars in the American flag. The alteration triggered loud complaints, and the uniforms were ultimately changed. The company also created controversy with its hyper-competitive Olympic slogan: "You Don't Win Silver—You Lose Gold."

In 1998, Nike seemed to hit a wall, as its overall revenues dropped off by eight percent.

Tiger Woods's $105-million Nike contract in 2000 was the largest endorsement deal ever signed by an athlete.

Sales in the Asian market, a region that couldn't get enough of Nike products in the past, fell sharply. Nike sold 50 percent of the athletic shoes purchased worldwide in 1998, but that was a lower percentage than the company had enjoyed the year before. The problem, Knight believed, was that Nike had gotten too big too fast and had become inefficient. To remedy the problem, Nike laid off 1,200 employees and reduced the company's annual operating costs by almost $200 million.

Yet perhaps the most damaging blow Nike took in the late 1990s was the public accusation that the company mistreated its overseas

As an official outfitter and a pioneer in performance apparel,
Nike has been prominently represented in recent Olympics

employees. Nike had several hundred factories around the world by then, mostly in Asia, where operating costs were lower. News reports revealed that many of these factories were "sweatshops" that paid their workers below-scale wages; in 1996, for example, in Indonesia, a country that manufactured 70 million pairs of shoes a year, thousands of workers made less than $2.50 a day. Overseas managers sometimes hired employees as young as 14 years old, and it was also brought to light that many Nike factories used dangerous chemicals in the manufacturing process without installing proper equipment to improve employee safety.

Faced with these serious charges, Knight acted quickly to minimize the damage. Issuing an equally public response, he pledged in 1998 to change company policies to ensure that Nike employees at overseas factories would be treated fairly, that the company would establish a minimum hiring age in its factories, and that Nike would tighten air-quality standards at the sites. "These moves do more than

"From Bowerman's Waffle Trainer to the Tour Accuracy golf ball, we make every effort to take consumers where they want to go before they realize they want to go there."

Phil Knight

Niketowns, located throughout the world,
average more than 30,000 square feet (2,790 sq m) per store

LEBRON JAMES

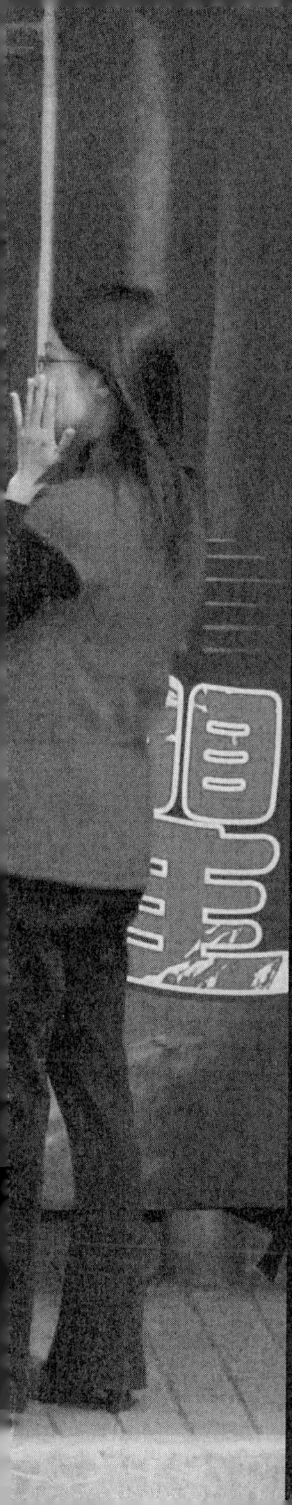

Nike Abroad

Although Nike was born in the U.S., the company didn't turn into a true giant until it started branching into foreign nations. The company entered its first foreign market, Canada, in 1972 and expanded operations to Australia in 1974. In 1977, Nike lined up distributorships in Asia and did the same in South America in 1978. In the first years of the 21st century, sales of footwear and apparel to customers in foreign markets made up an increasingly larger share of Nike's revenues, and by 2007, the company was selling its products in more than 150 countries. The statistics below show the global distribution of Nike's earnings during the 2007 fiscal year.

Total revenue:	$16.3 billion
United States:	$6.1 billion
Europe:	$4.7 billion
Asia:	$2.3 billion
*Americas:	$953 million
Other:	$2.2 billion

* (not including the U.S.)

Source: 2007 Nike Annual Report

just set industry standards," he said. "They reflect who we are as a company."

In the first few years of the 21st century, Nike slowly rebounded from the 1998 setback. By 2002, the company's revenues had crept up to $9.9 billion. A $5,000 share from Blue Ribbon Sports' early days was now worth more than $30 million. During these years, most of the company's growth occurred outside the U.S. Knight had long dreamed of turning Nike into a truly global corporation, and rising sales in Europe, Asia, and South America were proof of the company's ever-expanding reach. Since 1990, Nike had been opening superstores called Niketowns throughout the U.S. and the world. The stores, essentially enormous showrooms, sold a vast array of company products, including virtually every current model of Nike athletic shoe, and featured basketball courts and giant statues of sports heroes. By 2007, there were Niketowns doing brisk business in such foreign locations as London and Hong Kong.

Nike also addressed the stagnant growth of the late '90s by tapping into new corners of the sports world. The company expanded its All Conditions Gear (ACG) line of products designed for outdoor pursuits such as hiking, kayaking, and biking. In 1994, Nike had bought into hockey in a big way by acquiring Bauer, a leading manufacturer of hockey equipment and apparel. In 2002, the company entered the world of skateboarding, surfing, and snowboarding by making the Hurley International company a subsidiary, thereby adding apparel for these "alternative" sports to the Nike family.

5
Taking on the World

As Nike's offerings grew, so did its sports technology innovations. In 2000, Nike took its Air system to another level with Nike Shox, a sole technology that used a springy, resilient foam for cushioning. That same year, the company unveiled a groundbreaking line of formfitting body suits.

Given such names as the Swift Suit and Swift Spin, they were the result of years of research and testing in wind tunnels. By carefully combining an array of lightweight, elastic fibers, Nike's design team created a "second skin" that made athletes' bodies more aerodynamic. Different suits were made specifically for sprinters, speedskaters, swimmers, cyclists, and other athletes whose goal was to go as fast as possible, and the suits could be seen on such Olympic heroes as Australian sprinter Cathy Freeman and U.S. speed skater Apolo Anton Ohno in the years that followed.

In 2003, Nike made big headlines twice. First, it purchased Converse for $305 million. Converse was a shoe company with a 95-year history, and although it had never been a serious rival to Nike, it was a popular brand known for its "old-school" canvas basketball shoes. Then, only weeks later, Nike signed basketball phenomenon LeBron James to a seven-year, $90-million endorsement deal. Although James was only 18 years old (and about to jump straight from high school into the

NBA), he was widely seen as the "next Michael Jordan," and many industry experts thought he might one day become the first billion-dollar athlete in the world through his basketball and endorsement contracts. "Nike is the right fit and has the right product for me," said the 6-foot-8 "King James," who was given his own signature Nike collection.

Nike was again scoring big, but there were stumbles along the way. In 2004, Knight stepped down as the company's chief executive officer (CEO) and handed the reins to William Perez, formerly the CEO of S. C. Johnson & Son, a household-products company. But Perez's tenure was short. The new CEO wanted to break away from Nike's tradition of spending big dollars on advertising, and he and Knight, now company chairman, soon clashed. By early 2006, Perez would be asked to resign and would be replaced by Nike executive Mark Parker.

A more public bump in the road emerged in 2006, when Adidas, Nike's longtime rival,

Speed skater Apolo Anton Ohno won two Olympic medals in 2002 wearing Nike's Swift Skin suit purchased Reebok. Suddenly, Nike's two top challengers were turned into a single, powerful competitor. Although Nike made nearly $15 billion in 2006, soccer powerhouse Adidas brought in a formidable $9.5 billion and was determined to continue narrowing the gap. Nike had largely ignored soccer—the most popular sport in the world outside of the U.S.—during its first four decades, but that would change. The company had capitalized on the jogging boom of the 1970s, the basketball heyday of the 1980s, and the cross-training craze of the 1990s. Now, it resolved to make deep inroads into the world of soccer.

The longstanding and intense rivalry between Nike and Adidas is most evident today on soccer fields

In 2006, Nike took a major step in that direction by signing Brazilian star Ronaldinho, the best soccer player in the world, to his own signature collection. (Two years before, Nike had inked Freddy Adu, a 14-year-old American soccer whiz, to a $1-million contract.) Nike also spent more than $100 million on advertising during the 2006 World Cup soccer tournament, while Adidas spent close to $200 million. Adidas had built its name on the sport of soccer, and it made clear that Nike was going to face a tough fight to claim that throne. "Soccer is the lifeblood and the backbone of our brand," said Adidas executive Erich Stamminger.

"There's no way either one would even approach Nike, much less overtake them, on their own. This new, combined entity has a chance to make a run. Now, it's game on."

Advertising Executive Jon Hickey On the 2006 Merger of Adidas and Reebok

In dollars, athletes, and advertisements,
Nike today intends to remain the biggest and the best

At Home in Oregon

In 2007, *Fortune* magazine listed Nike at number 69 on its "100 Best Companies to Work For" list. In giving the company such praise, the magazine stressed Nike's unique workplace atmosphere and facilities: "The Oregon campus is a sporting paradise with tennis courts, indoor and outdoor tracks, soccer fields, running trails, two sports centers, and an 11-lane pool used for swimming, scuba, and kayaking lessons." Indeed, Nike's "World Campus" headquarters, which opened in Beaverton, Oregon, in 1990, represents rare success and a singular vision. The facility, which originally covered 74 acres (30 ha) and has since more than doubled in size, is surrounded by woods and features running paths, lakes, and high-tech fitness centers. Buildings on the sprawling campus are named after famous "Nike athletes" such as tennis great John McEnroe, basketball legend Michael Jordan, and cycling hero Lance Armstrong, and the company issues bonuses to those employees who bike to work rather than drive.

"It's very, very emotional for us."

By 2007, Nike employed about 29,000 people, but the company had plans to go even bigger—much bigger. In February of that year, Mark Parker announced that Nike intended to make $23 billion a year by 2011. To do this, the company planned to grow in all phases, but especially to branch into soccer and to expand operations in countries such as Russia, India, and Brazil, each of which, Nike believed, could soon become a billion-dollar market. "As the market leader, we have the ability and the responsibility to take the industry and our partners to a new and better place," Parker said. "Our vision is clear. I've never been more excited about our opportunities."

Nike, the little shoe distributor from Oregon that grew to span the world as a sports apparel empire, has long had more than its share of supporters and detractors. Nike loyalists admire the innovation, vision, and competitive spirit that have made the company famous, while critics decry the high-priced, "premium product" philosophy that they say makes Nike big bucks while ignoring or mistreating people of low income. But what no one can dispute is that the company with the Swoosh is today king in the world of sports, and it plans to stay in power for a long time.

Glossary

ad campaign a series of advertisements with a common theme

aerodynamic able to move through air or water with very little resistance

commission money paid to salespeople by their employer as a percentage of their sales

distributor an individual or company that sells and delivers another company's product to retail stores

endorsements business deals in which a well-known person is paid to express approval of a product

exclusive contract an agreement between two parties in which they promise to do business only with each other in a given market

fiscal year a 12-month schedule by which a company keeps records of its earnings; it differs by company and usually does not correspond to the calendar year

importer someone who buys products in a foreign country in order to sell them in his or her own country

innovation a new idea or way of doing something

investors people who put money into a company; their money grows if the company is financially successful

laid off dismissed (as employees) not because of poor individual performance but because a company is seeking to save money

latex a substance found in various plants that is used to make rubber and some plastics

line of credit an agreement to lend money, or supply credit, to an individual or company

luge a sport in which a person rides a small sled down a chute while lying flat on his or her back, trying to complete the "run" in the fastest time possible

market a geographic region or segment of the population to which companies try to sell goods; for example, the North American market, the youth market, or the world market

promote to encourage the use of a product among consumers by explaining its benefits

royalty a share of a product's proceeds paid to someone in exchange for an endorsement or other valuable contribution

signature something that is unique to a certain person and is often given distinctive or easily recognizable features

stock shared ownership in a company by many people who buy shares, or portions, of stock, hoping the company will make a profit and the stock value will increase

subsidiary a company that retains its own name but is entirely controlled by another company

traction the ability of an object to grip a surface; the texture of a shoe's sole, for example, can keep a runner from slipping

trademark a symbol or name that belongs legally and exclusively to one company; it may also refer to something that is unique about a company

Selected Bibliography

Goldman, Robert, and Stephen Papson. *Nike Culture: The Sign of the Swoosh.* Thousand Oaks, Calif.: Sage Publications, 1999.

Katz, Donald R. *Just Do It: The Nike Spirit in the Corporate World.* New York: Random House, 1994.

Klein, Naomi. *No Logo: Taking Aim at the Brand Bullies.* Toronto: Knopf Canada, 2000.

LaFeber, Walter. *Michael Jordan and the New Global Capitalism.* New York: W. W. Norton and Company, 1999.

Moore, Kenny. *Bowerman and the Men of Oregon: The Story of Oregon's Legendary Coach and Nike's Co-founder.* New York: Rodale Books, 2006.

Strasser, J. B., and Laurie Becklund. *The Unauthorized Story of Nike and the Men Who Played There.* New York: Harcourt Brace, 1991.

Index